Chapter 1

The Beginning

Little Speedy Jo showed up one spring day, all wet and all legs. Her first day was a wonder. Mom kept saying, "Come on Speedy, get up, let's go. From this day forward you will be called Speedy, Speedy Jo, Little Speedy Jo, so try harder, we have got to get moving." But poor Speedy Jo was all legs, twisted, crossed and gangly. But Mom persisted, "Come on Speedy, get under those legs and stand up." On and on this went for what seemed like forever for Jo, but finally there she was, up on all fours. Uneasy, but up, and oh so proud of herself.

"Lunch time, hon," said Mom. Oh, and how hungry a young pronghorn could get after all that exercise! Lunch was good, then a nap. When Speedy awoke from her nap, Mom said, "Speedy, I'm going to hide you now and leave you for a while. I must eat for both of us, and will be gone to the sweet grass for a short time. I won't be far away."

"Get up, get up," said Speedy to her mom. "Now go hide and wait. This makes no sense to me, Mom. Don't be gone too long please, Mom. Come back right away, please," Speedy begged.

"Well, yes Speedy, I'll be back as quick as I can," Mom replied. Mom then explained, "I'm sorry I have to hide you, but it will take about a week until you get stronger, then we will join the band. It's not going to be easy, Speedy, but it's the way it's been done forever. You have to be strong so you can keep up. I know you can do it, and please be patient and strong, and no matter what, don't panic."

Speedy Jo said nothing but a subdued, "Okay."

How strange and scary this is, thought Speedy, to be tucked away and left alone in a patch of dry grass from last year with young green grass from this spring all intertwined together. What if Mom didn't come back? How frightening this was for a day-old pronghorn.

Speedy's hiding place was largely made up of an old stand of needle grass, blue stem, some wild rye and a small yucca. A locust flew over head making a fluttering noise, like two hand fans being rubbed together. Speedy froze at the sound. A ruby throated humming bird buzzed around a wild daisy gathering nectar, then was off to another. Speedy settled down a little, but she was so tense.

The day wore on. The sun was high in the sky and so nice and warm along with a gentle breeze. Speedy was feeling more relaxed when a shadow began to cover her hiding place, making Speedy very nervous and scared. Her breathing almost came to a stop. She hugged the ground, closed her eyes, and wondered where Mom was. Speedy opened her eyes but continued to be still. The shadow moved by but then another came, then another. Speedy was so frightened, for she was no bigger than a house cat. A grunting and snorting sound seemed to follow along with the shadows, which turned out to be four young male bison, swishing flies, throwing dust and sparring with each other as they cropped grass, passing only inches away from Speedy's hiding place.

When the four young bison had finally moved on, Speedy breathed a little easier. The young bison had come so close to Speedy that the grass was trampled just inches from where she was lying.

As the day wore on, Speedy watched the grass that had been smashed down, slowly start to rise and return to its original state. Speedy thought, how neat and how much safer for me.

When evening came that first day, the nighthawks came out to catch flying insects. When the nighthawks would swoop down after insects, it made a heavy vacuum swishing sound, which just scared Speedy half to death. She wanted to get up and run, but she held fast. Then to her relief, she heard Mom's voice from behind her. "Speedy, Speedy Jo, it is Mom. Time to eat, hon," she called.

Speedy was so happy and so hungry! "Oh, Mom, you came back!" Speedy exclaimed.

Speedy's Mom replied, "Of course I came back." She asked, "What did you think I would do? Tell me, how was your day?"

While eating, Speedy filled Mom in on the happenings of her day. Mom listened as she washed her baby. Later, Mom put Speedy to bed and then went to sleep a few yards from where Speedy lay. She was so very watchful through the night.

The next morning, Speedy had breakfast, and Mom hid her once again. Off went Mom, and Speedy Jo's second day was about to begin. Mom warned Speedy to watch up above for the golden eagles who are always on the lookout, and not to underestimate Mr. Red Tail Hawk.

Later on that morning, a wind came up and bent over the grass in front of Speedy, giving her a view of her world and what lay ahead for her. The taller grasses swayed and waved in the wind like waves on an ocean.

The view from Speedy's hiding place was so exciting. Out there lay bluffs, buttes, rolling hills, mesas, canyons, gullies and the high plains. A creek snaked its way through the plains and around hills and valleys and slowly disappeared into the great expanse of the plains. Stands of cottonwoods, elms, willows and wild plum trees grew along its banks. The larger gullies were dotted with chokecherry trees and a lonesome cottonwood here and there.

Along the bluffs and buttes stood pinion pine and Jack pine. Buck brush also grew thick in spots, along with grasses, boulders and rocks that were strewn in every direction. All the different colors from the leaves of the trees added to the beauty of spring. The plains looked like a green carpet made up of buffalo grass, gamma grass and a little blue stem grass. Flowers showed their

Anne M Martin

faces in all corners of the plains. The air was filled with the smell of sage: silver sage, sand sage, fringed sage, and the big sage brush, salt sage or winter sage.

Prickly pear cactus patches were everywhere with crowns of yellow flowers. A few little barrel cacti with their purple flowers popped up here and there. Yucca grew along the side of small hills. The very fragrant western yarrow filled the air with its sweet smell of domed white flowers.

Bison were everywhere. The antelope bands intermingled with them. Mule deer were browsing along the bluffs. A few elk roamed the mesas and higher hills. A small herd of mustangs were down by the creek, drinking and playing in the water.

Buffalo wallows were a common sight. It seemed they were in use all the time. The buffalo were rolling in the dust and mud, or rubbing their heads on the sides of the wallows trying to rid themselves of flies and lice.

The night brought the moon and stars out. The coyotes started to howl, sing and cackle all through the night. An old prairie wolf also joined in while crickets and katydids sang their songs. Then a mountain lion let out with a scream on a mesa off in the distance as if to say, "Quiet out there." And silence did fall over the area. Everything fell silent. Even the mild wind seemed to become still, but only for a short time, then all would start up again. A great horned owl called to

his mate down by the creek. The mate called back and they finally joined up and were together.

On Speedy's third day, after a much-needed lunch, Mom moved her over to a big sagebrush. "Get under there, Speedy, and stay put," Mother directed. She added, "I'll be back this evening. Love you, hon."

Speedy's stay under the big sagebrush was interesting and kind of fun. First, a stinkbug came along, stopped to look Speedy over, raised up on his haunches and let off a very nasty odor. Poor Speedy. She had to endure this and stay put at the same time. Off scampered the stinkbug, leaving poor Speedy to wait for a breeze to freshen the air. At last a mild breeze, along with the thick dark clouds, rolled across the sky.

It started to rain that evening. The raindrops made tap, tap, tick, tick sounds when it hit the branches of the big sage. The air was cool and fresh. Lightning danced across the sky, with some coming down to earth, bright silver and gold in color. Thunder rumbled and slammed through the night. Even the ground seemed to shake. The cloud-covered sky turned Speedy's world into total darkness. Only when lightning bolts flashed across the sky was there light.

Speedy was so frightened. The wind picked up and made a moaning sound like something in pain. The rain kept falling and some drops worked their way through the branches of the big sage, falling on Speedy. Speedy was getting very hungry and scared. A voice called out, "Speedy! Speedy, are you okay little one?" It was not Mom's voice. Speedy did not answer. "It's your Great Aunt Myrt," said the voice. "Your mom sent me over here to stay with you. She was caught on the other side of a dry riverbed, and with all the rain, the river is flooding. She will be back tomorrow morning. I can't help with supper, so it will be a long night, hon. Now, if you are there, answer me," Aunt Myrt instructed.

All Speedy said was, "I'm hungry."

Aunt Myrt replied, "I know, Speedy. Try and sleep. It will make the night go faster. I'll be right here."

Poor little Speedy was not only getting a little wet, she was starving, but the fearless, feisty voice from behind gave Speedy enough courage to make it through that long, stormy night.

Finally morning came. What a wonderful sight. The clouds were gone and there to the east the sun started to rise. To Speedy's relief, stood Mom talking to Aunt Myrt.

"Well Speedy, do you want breakfast?" asked Mom. "Hurry hon. All is clear."

Speedy shot out from under the brush like a flash of lightning.

"Easy Speedy. There's more where that came from," Mom said reassuringly. Speedy was starved.

Aunt Myrt said, "the kid is fast isn't she? Well, I've got to run."

Speedy felt so good to have a full stomach again and such a warm and safe feeling to have Mom back. Mom cleaned Speedy up and they talked a while. Speedy couldn't help noticing it, "Wow! Mom, what's that in the sky? It is so beautiful, oh Mom," Speedy was so overwhelmed with what she saw.

"It's a rainbow, Speedy. They show up with the rain—sometimes during, sometimes after—they are pretty, that's for sure."

"Wow!" said Speedy again, as though she was under a spell.

Then Mom hid Speedy back under the big sagebrush. Speedy was so content and cozy now, and getting sleepy. Speedy felt secure knowing that Mom was close by.

But sleep was not yet to be part of Speedy's morning, for here came a column of black ants marching through, right past Speedy's nose and some even marching right over her nose, which tickled. All of a sudden Speedy heard, "Slurp, slurp, slurp. Ah, yummy." And then a small "burp." To Speedy's relief, a horned toad appeared, all smiles, and what a chatter box.

The horned toad said, "Hi there young pronghorn. Your mom hid you good, didn't she? My name is Humphrey. I just love these black ants. Yum, yum. They're so sweet and juicy. Those darn red ants are nasty. Too much acid gives me heartburn and indigestion. They bite, too." Humphrey told Speedy, "hold still young lope. I'll snip those right off your nose." Slurp, slurp. The horned toad's tongue quickly removed the ants from Speedy's nose.

"Looks like these tasty ants are running out," observed Humphrey. "Oh well, I am full to the gills anyway. I need a nap to sleep off my meal." He continued, "Sure was a nice rain. Freshened things up a little. Of course, when it cools down, I get a little stiff."

Speedy couldn't help but smile at the little horned toad.

Humphrey asked, "you don't mind if I slip under this branch and take a snooze, do you?"

"Go ahead," Speedy replied. With a burp and a groan the horned toad went into a very comfortable sleep. Speedy just smiled and had to hold back from laughing at Humphrey. Soon the night fell upon the plains with a red and gold sunset. How beautiful thought Speedy.

The next day, Speedy awoke and the horned toad was gone. Mom was on time with lunch, being very careful to make sure no danger was close by before giving Speedy her meal.

"Soon we will join the band," Mom informed Speedy. "You have done well, hon. I'll be back this evening, so stay put."

"How much longer, Mom?" asked Speedy.

"Not much longer hon, be patient just a little longer and I'll see you tonight. You have so much courage Speedy, and I love you so. Until tonight, bye, bye."

A bullsnake slithered by, took a look at Speedy, poked its tongue out and asked if she had seen any mice in the area.

"Why?" asked Speedy.

"Well, why do you think?" snapped the bullsnake.

Speedy replied, "Well, I haven't seen any mice. I don't even know what mice are. I'm barely a week old."

The bullsnake said, "Oh, why should I waste my time with you, lope?" Off went the bullsnake. What a difference thought Speedy, between the horned toad and the bullsnake. Speedy wondered where her mom was.

Evening came at last, bringing Mom and supper. Speedy told Mom about the bullsnake and what an unfriendly sort he was. "They're that way at times," said Mom. "He might have had a bad morning. You are not to worry about it."

"Okay," said Speedy.

After supper Speedy had her bath, then was tucked away in bed. Mom bedded down a few yards from Speedy's hiding place. Night soon fell on the plains.

Finally, one day Mom said, "Well, hon, I'm taking you to our band. You're strong enough now and wiser."

Speedy and her mom showed up at the band and all gathered around them. They welcomed Speedy and told her mom how adorable and lovable she was. Speedy's Great Aunt Myrt gave her a stern look. She said to Speedy, "I see you survived your first week." She continued, "Well, little one, you listen to your mom and take heed to what she tells you. Do you understand me?"

"Yes," Speedy replied.

There beside his mom stood Jasper, Speedy's friend-to-be in their future adventures of growing up.

Early the next day, Mom said to Speedy, "Well, time to get a move on, Jo." This time Little Speedy Jo was ready to go, no problem. Up and away she went, right along with Mom. "My goodness," Speedy said to Mom, "sure is a big country."

It's the plains, hon," said Mom. "Now you listen and learn quick, dear girl, because you cannot make any mistakes out here. You've been given great speed, a keen eye and good hearing, so use them to their fullest."

"Okay, Mom."

"Good," said Mom. "A willing student. Let's get moving."

Little Speedy Jo thought we sure do move a lot, always on the go.

As the summer progressed, Jo's schooling increased; like when she laid down on a prickly pear cactus patch and Mom had to remove the stickers; or when a rattler introduced himself in a not-so-friendly way; or the grumpy old badger who scolded Jo for getting too close to his den; or where to hide from lightning storms; or which side of a hill or bluff to stay on in a wind or bad rain; or what water to drink and what not to eat. Jo could really run, getting faster and faster.

One day Mom, Jo and the rest of the small band came to a brush thicket. All went through but Jo. Mom said, "Hon, lower your head, fold your front legs and dive through the opening." Jo did, and to her surprise she made it without leaving one hair on a twig. She was pretty darn proud of herself. Jo and her friends would play tag all day long, and prance and bound.

One day the sky became very dark and cloudy. The wind came up, and lightning struck the plains. A fire broke out and the wind proceeded with great speed across the plains. Ming, the leader of the band, let out a snort and warned everyone to run for Lost Canyon. With all

Anne Martin

haste, poor Jo, the smallest of the group, was in a nervous dither, "Mom! Mom! Where's Mom?"

Speedy Jo heard Mom calling, "Run, Jo! Run as fast as you can so we don't get caught in the fire!"

So away they went. Jo had run and played all summer, but not like this. "Run, Speedy Jo, run! Put your head down and run!" Poor little Jo was falling behind and the fire was closing in. Little Jo couldn't even hear Mom's calls now with the roar of the fire and wind. So, little Jo had a great fear come over her. A fear she did not like at all. Then a great burst of what she did not know boiled up inside her, and she lowered her head, opened her mouth, and put herself into high road gear and away she went!

She heard herself say, "Run, Speedy Jo, run! Run, run, run," and run she did—through smoke and more smoke and dust. Where did dust come from? Oh, well. Into the mouth of the canyon she flew and to her surprise, she was the only one there. So she pranced around and waited, and then all of a sudden the rest of the band showed up with Ming bringing up the rear, making sure everyone was accounted for. To all their surprise, there stood little Speedy Jo. The band surrounded Jo in total admiration, and Mom, bless her heart, was so proud of her Speedy Jo.

"Mom," Jo said, "where have you been? I've been waiting for you."

"Oh, Jo," Mom said. "I'm so proud of you and love you so much. I knew when I named you Speedy Jo, I named you right, my sweet little Speedy Jo."

Chapter 2

Speedy Jo's First Summer

On a clear June day, Speedy and her pal, Jasper, were exploring not far from the band when they came across a large stand of wild flowers. Jasper said, "Boy, they sure are pretty, Speedy."

"Oh, aren't they though, Jasper! They smell so lovely!" Speedy went over to take a sniff, when all of a sudden a nasty old bumblebee gave Speedy a quick and painful sting.

"Hey!" screamed Speedy, and away she ran with Jasper following close behind. "Mom! Mom!" screamed Speedy with tears running down from her eyes. "My nose, Mom! My nose, it hurts!" Speedy's nose had already swollen.

"Oh, Speedy, come here. Let's have a look. Looks like Mr. Bumble Bee nailed you good. Come along."

Jasper followed. They came to a small seep. Mom said, "Now Speedy, kind of kneel down and put your nose in the mud."

"What?" said Speedy. "Put my nose in the mud?"

"Yes, Speedy," said Mom.

"But Mom, it smells!"

"Oh, the smell will leave. Either the smell or the pain, so come along and get it over with."

Jasper just stood and took it all in, eyes as big as moons. So Speedy held her breath and put her little black nose in the mud. "Oh, Mom, It's cold!"

"Good," said Mom. "Feel better?"

"Yes, Mom."

"Rub it good now, hon."

So Speedy did. All day long little Speedy worked her nose in the mud and all her pals watched. Toward evening, Speedy's nose was almost back down to normal size. Even though she had this stale, mucky odor to her, all her friends laughed when she walked by with a glob of mud on her nose. Speedy just giggled.

"Go to bed, Speedy."

"Now Mom? The sun is still up."

"Now," said Mom.

The summer nights shown light with the big moon and the sky just exploded with millions of stars. Speedy thought, how truly wonderful it all was.

Speedy watched an argument between a pair of kangaroo rats. Mrs. K was scolding Mr. K for not keeping their yard spotless while she was away. Speedy smiled at how Mr. K took his scolding and remained calm and held his composure, not saying a word, but "Yes, Dear. No, Dear." Finally, to Speedy's relief the pair went inside their home and there was some peace and quiet again.

The next day, Speedy was up at dawn and went to roust Jasper. "Get up, Jasper."

"It's early, Speedy. I want to stay put."

"Oh, get up you lazy thing. Let's explore!"

"Can't it wait until later?"

"Oh, you are the laziest thing."

"Oh, all right. Where?"

"Down by the creek," said Speedy. Off they went. Dew hung on the grass and brush. "Boy, Jasper, doesn't it smell wonderful?"

"What?" said Jasper.

"The freshness of the morning."

"I bet it would smell just as good later on in the day."

"Jasper, you're impossible."

When they reached the creek, a small fog rose above the water. Jasper said. "That sure looks kind of spooky."

"It's beautiful, Jasper," said Speedy.

A small fish jumped and made a circle in the water. "Let's get closer, Jasper." Speedy and Jasper went on down to the edge of the creek. "Listen to the water talk, Jasper."

"Talk?" said Jasper. "It's just running over those rocks out there."

"No, it's talking to us, Jasper."

"Well then what is it saying, if you're so smart?"

"It's telling where it's going and where it's been."

"Well, that's nice, Speedy, that water can talk to you and you understand what it says."

"Oh, you're impossible, Jasper."

Jasper noticed it first. "Speedy, look over there, something with two heads!" It was a young

Indian brave on a beautiful pinto pony. "What should we do, Speedy?"

"Well, let's wait and see." Said Speedy.

"No," said Jasper, "I'm leaving now." Then Jasper slipped and fell into the creek. Poor Jasper. He became stuck in a mud bank. The more he tried to free himself, the more he became mired in the creek mud. Jasper just squealed because he was so frightened.

Speedy said, "Take it easy, Jasper."

The young brave heard the commotion and came their way.

"What's going to happen to me, Speedy?"

"Nothing," Speedy said. "We'll get you out."

Speedy looked up and on the other side of the creek stood the young brave astride his beautiful pony. Speedy just stared but she could not run away from Jasper's dilemma. She held fast. The young brave crossed over to their side. Jasper was so very scared.

The young brave dismounted and walked to where Jasper was. A smile spread across the face of the young brave. He quickly admired the bravery of Speedy, for she held her ground and did not leave her friend.

"Oh little brave one," said the young Indian boy. Speedy came close to the brave as if to say, "please help my friend Jasper." The young brave held out his hand to Speedy and said, "I'm called Lone Eagle. I will help your little friend out of the mud."

Speedy touched the hand of Lone Eagle with her nose, and a bond was formed at that moment. Lone Eagle waded into the mud and gently lifted Jasper from bondage and put him back on the bank. Lone Eagle crawled back up the bank and cleaned the mud from Jasper. No matter what he tried, Jasper was so scared he could not move.

Lone Eagle stood Jasper up after cleaning and washing him. Speedy came up and watched, her eyes filled with great caring. Lone Eagle could not help noticing the caring in this young Lope. Lone Eagle said, "Go now, return to your band, and be careful where you jump and play."

Off went Jasper, leaving Speedy with Lone Eagle. Speedy looked up at Lone Eagle. The young brave bent down and patted Speedy behind the ears. Speedy pawed at Lone Eagle's moccasins with a great thank you.

"Go now, little brave one. All is well."

Lone Eagle mounted his pony and Speedy pranced up a small hill. They looked at each other. Lone Eagle waved goodbye to Speedy. Speedy bobbed her head. Off rode Lone Eagle, and Speedy watched until the young brave disappeared into the horizon.

Summer wore on. The heat on the plains can be so intense. One day out of the clear blue, Speedy asked Mom, "Why is it either too dry, too wet, too hot, or too cold where we live?"

Speedy's remark brought a smile to Mom's face. "Speedy is sounding like a veteran of the

plains at such a young age. Well, what can I say, Speedy? It's the plains, hon, you'll have to get used to it."

"Well, I'll sure try, Mom," said Speedy.

"Speedy, at times you can be so ornery," Mom said.

They both broke out with heart-felt laughter. Speedy thought it was great to laugh with Mom, and Mom with her. It drew them closer together. The band would stand in circles with the young lying under them for shade. Speedy was always in wonder of her world, and very caring of all things around her.

One day when out romping, she came across a pup coyote. "Hi, my name is Eddy. What is your name?"

"I'm Speedy Jo," she answered.

Eddy said, "I've been told not to talk to you for some reason."

"Oh, why not?" asked Speedy.

"I really don't know," said Eddy. "It's just what I was told. Mom said later I would find out."

"Oh, Eddy, let's be friends," said Jo.

"Well, I guess we could," said Eddy. "We're all just young ones anyway. I've been practicing my howling. Do you want to hear some of it?"

"Sure," said Jo.

So Eddy started off. Jo was a little startled. "Oh my, that's pretty good, Eddy."

"Well thanks, Jo."

About that time Eddy's mom appeared. Jo kind of got a funny feeling, which wasn't to her liking. Eddy's mom snarled and barked at Eddy to come home at once. Jo's sense told her it was time to get back to the band in quick time.

"Bye Jo!"

"Bye Eddy!"

Jo ran right out of there as fast as she could. When Jo returned home, Mom said, "Where have you been?"

"Oh, I made a new friend. His name is Eddy Coyote."

"What?" said Mom. "Have you lost your little mind? You are not to leave the band any more. Do you understand me? And no back talk. You stand over there by that sage brush and don't you move!"

"Oh Mom!"

"Get!"

"Okay, Mom."

Little Speedy stuck it out and finally Jasper showed up to play, bringing with him his new neighbor.

"Judy, this is Speedy Jo. She outruns fires, talks to water and to two-headed things."

"Oh Jasper, be quiet. Hi Judy."

"Hi, Jo."

Judy was a shy young lope, but friendly.

"Mom, can we play?"

"Well, all right, but not too far and watch who you talk to."

Off they went playing tag and racing. Down to the creek they ran. Like all young animals, poor Judy saw her reflection in the water for the first time, and jumped back. Speedy and Jasper just giggled.

"There's an antelope fawn in the water, we have to save it!" said Judy.

"Judy, it's you."

"Me?"

"Yes, you. Go look again."

So Judy eased on up to the creek and slowly peered into the water, and just stared for the longest time. Then she too started to giggle. They all laughed and decided to run up a small butte and look over the country.

Away they ran. On the way, they saw this freshly dug pile of dirt. "Hey, let's jump over it and see who can jump the farthest," said Speedy.

Over they went. One, then the other two. All of a sudden a grumpy, cantankerous old badger came out of his hole. "Hey, can't you young lopes play some other place? You're causing dirt to roll down in my home and I'm trying to catch a nap. It's bad enough when some lamebrain buffalo uses my roof for a dust bath. Now you three have to use it for jumping games. NOW GET!"

"We're sorry, Mr. Badger. We'll run along."

"Good," said the badger. "And don't come back. The name is Henry and don't forget it."

Off they went, heading for the butte. "Boy, he sure wasn't very nice," said Judy.

"Oh, we'll just stay clear of him," Speedy said.

"Good idea," Jasper added.

But in her heart Speedy thought Henry must need a friend.

They ran up the butte for all they were worth, and giggled when they reached the top. "Wow," said Speedy. "Just look out there. Isn't it just great?"

"Oh, it sure is, Speedy," said Judy and Jasper.

The three took in the view for quite some time. "Well, we better head back. It's going to get dark soon."

Off they went, and all of a sudden a rasping, rattling noise sounded. The closer they came, the louder it got. Finally, a voice said, "that's far enough. I can't see very well, but I know there are three of you." Out from under the shelf of a rock slithered a very large rattler. "You're in my area," he said. "I don't like it!"

"We are sorry, Mr. Rattler. We're just three young lopes out having fun, and we're heading back home. We didn't mean to anger you."

"Well I'm always kind of angry. If you were deaf, half blind and spent your whole life with a ground level view of the world, you wouldn't be too happy either."

"We're sorry. I'm Speedy, this is Judy and Jasper."

"Well, my name is Walter," said the rattler. "I'm sorry I had to scold you. I would just as soon be left alone and go my way, so you three better run along."

Off they went, back to the band.

They met many of their neighbors that summer. Ferrets, horned toads, ground squirrels, foxes, bobcats, prairie dogs, bullsnakes, hog nose snakes, hawks, prairie chickens, birds of all kinds, muskrats in the creeks and slews, kangaroo rats, all the creatures of the plains, and of course, Mr. Skunk and Jasper's rude introduction.

One cool cloudy summer day, Speedy, Judy and Jasper were out running and racing when they decided to crash through a brush pile for some new game. So, they decided boys first. Jasper said, "Whoever gets through the brush the easiest wins."

Off he went, head down, full blast ahead. They didn't know that old Pete, the bachelor skunk, had made a home in there.

Jasper had just hit the brush and startled Pete, so Pete let fly. Poor Jasper slammed on the brakes and backed out so fast, right into a large yucca bush. First he let out with an "ooh," then an "owe."

The smell was a bit much, but Speedy and Judy just laughed themselves silly. Poor Jasper had to spend the next few days by himself, far away from everyone. Plus he had to contend with the sore back end!   Old Pete came by to apologize to Jasper for the accident, and tried to make things right, and all was forgiven.

About a week later, after Jasper had completely aired out, Speedy, Jasper and Judy were out racing as fast as they could, saying to one another, "Go-go-go."   They zoomed up this sandstone outcropping and came to a screeching halt.   There was a shear drop-off right in front of them.

"That was a close one," said Judy.

Jasper thought that maybe they should check out the area first before running full blast ahead and finding out the hard way.

"What's wrong?" asked Speedy.   "Are we losing our sense of adventure?"   But Speedy had to agree.   No sense in anyone getting hurt, that was for sure.

Something up in the sky caught their attention.   Vultures were circling and slowly descending down to earth.   They heard a commotion further down in the ravine.

"Let's check it out," said Judy.

"Let's not," Jasper said.

They asked Speedy what she thought. "Boy, I don't know what we should do. I don't like the feel of this."

Up behind them came Aunt Myrt and her friend, Annabelle. "What, pray tell, are you three doing up here?" asked Aunt Myrt. "All three of

you are too far from the band, aren't you? she added.

No one said a word. Finally, Judy spoke up first. "What's going on down there?" she asked.

Annabelle answered, "You don't want to know."

"Why?" asked Speedy.

"Well," said Myrt, "maybe we should show them. They should know anyway. Ok, let's go have a look."

The five turned and went back down a slope toward the commotion. The closer they came, the louder the noise. Vultures were still coming down from the sky. They eased up behind a big sagebrush.

"Ok," said Aunt Myrt. "I hope the three of you are ready for this. Come and look through the branches."

So, they did. First Speedy, then Judy and finally Jasper. What they saw made them totally silent. Not a muscle was moving; frozen you might say; they were in total shock. Down below the sight was grizzly, but a natural thing in the way of nature on the plains. A bison had died, for it was his time. The coyotes were taking their share; a prairie wolf or two were in on the feast; the red foxes were waiting their turn; while the smaller swift and kit foxes hid in the brush waiting for a chance to grab some scraps. Under some of the hide crawled orange and black beetles, maggots were in certain parts that were torn away earlier, and flies buzzed all around. The vultures sat on rocks and on the ground waiting for their chance to feed. They were good at waiting. The air was foul. Magpies waited in trees near the site. A few crows showed up out of nowhere.

Aunt Myrt said, "Have you seen enough?" No one answered. The silence behind the brush was stifling. "Okay, let's go," Aunt Myrt said. She had to give Speedy a small poke to get her moving.

Slowly and silently they left and went back up the hill and when they reached the top, Myrt stopped the group. "Well, any questions?" No one said a word. Myrt said, "Life is not always running, playing and having fun, as the three of you have seen. Are you feeling a little sick?"

Even though Aunt Myrt seemed stern, cold and uncompassionate about what they had seen, her heart was aching on the inside for the three young ones. She knew the shock and hurt they felt and how frightening it was for them. She also knew how cruel and uncaring the world could be at times.

Although Myrt's heart was breaking, she kept her stern, firm way and tried to give Speedy, Jasper, and Judy some strength to look to. In her own way, Aunt Myrt was all love. She was true, honest and fair.

Annabelle said "Maybe we should head back. It is getting dark." Off they went. The only sound coming from the five was the sound of light hoof beats on the sod; not a word was spoken.

When they returned home, Speedy's mom said, "Where were you? Did you have fun this afternoon? What's wrong, Speedy?"

"Oh, I just don't feel well, Mom. I just want to lay down."

Aunt Myrt told Speedy's mom what they had seen. She said, "Maybe I shouldn't have, but it was a good lesson, a part of growing up. It will make them more alert and wiser to their world. Well, niece, I must get home. See you tomorrow. Tell Speedy goodnight for me and that I love her."

"Bye, bye," said Speedy's mom. Mom went to check on Speedy. "How are you feeling, hon?"

"Oh, I guess okay," said Speedy.

"Have you eaten?" Mom asked Speedy.

"No, I'm not hungry, Mom."

"Do you want to talk about what you saw?" asked Mom.

Speedy thought a while, then said, "Why do things like that have to happen? Couldn't someone have helped the buffalo? Doesn't anyone care? It makes me so mad. The poor buffalo was alone, Mom. No one stayed to help or tried to make the buffalo feel better." Tears started to show in Speedy's eyes and they ran down her cheeks, but she did not totally break down and cry. Her pride held her back.

"Oh Speedy," Mom said. "I see I have a very special little girl here. Let me try to explain. It was the buffalo's time, hon. It is the way nature works. It is called life. All things come to pass and go forward again, we have to carry on.

Sometimes the hurt is so great that you think you are going to die inside. But then in time, you look around, and there all around you is hope. Maybe it comes a little at a time, but it is there. Believe me, hon, please." Mom bedded down with Speedy that night to comfort her. Mom knew what a special and caring girl she had at her side. Speedy remained quiet all through the night, saying not one word.

The following week it clouded up and cut loose with a great downfall of rain, rain, and more rain. Ming made sure everyone was together behind a bluff and not down in a gully or wash, for they were overflowing with water. The dry riverbeds were at their brink with flooding, and the rain kept coming.

The antelope coat is made for any kind of weather, but the wet was starting to get to all of them. Some hail would fall and sting and bounce off them and off the ground. The very young would shelter under the mothers and aunts.

Finally, the storm broke and the sun came out. The following night, after the heavy rain, the little prairie frogs started to sing. They croaked all night long.

Speedy asked, "Mom, what is making that noise?"

Mom said, "Shh, quiet, those are what we call little Timmys. They come with the rain."

"Oh," Speedy said quietly.

"You go to sleep, hon," said Mom. Speedy just lay there listening to the endless croaking of the little frogs until sleep won her over.

After the heavy rain, every pothole, old buffalo wallow and dry riverbed holes were filled with water. About a week later, they came alive with tadpoles, tadpole shrimp, water bugs and critters that are hard to explain. Mother Nature was running her course. The plains just exploded with greenery and flowers. It looked like a giant lawn planted with a hundred kinds of flowers.

"You know what I feel like doing?" Speedy asked.

"What?" asked Jasper and Judy.

"I feel like singing!"

"Singing? What a wonderful idea,"

"Let's sing about the day, the night and everything around us," said Speedy. "Then we will dance."

"Dance! I can't dance," was Jasper's reply.

"There is nothing to it Jasper," Judy said. "Just get in the rhythm of the song!"

"Well I'm not going to do it!"

"Oh, don't be so difficult Jasper. Speedy and I will teach you."

"No way," said Jasper.

Speedy and Judy started to sing and then they began to dance. "Oh come on, Jasper, join in. Don't be an old poo!"

"Oh all right, but don't tell anyone." Jasper surprised the two little gals plus himself. He had

A very beautiful voice, and once he got into the swing of the dance, what a stepper!
The three friends sang this song:

SPEEDY'S SONG

Words by K.D. Ruff

Arranged by:
Si Travis
Sheila Kettering

1. Oh my how won-der-ful, and beau-ti-ful, ev-ry- thing is

The morn-ing sun ri-ses a new day be – gins.

The flowers and the grass-es,. the trees and the sage;

How they all come alive with the winds and the rains;
(repeat last time only)

How tru – ly wonderful life is on the plains.

2.   Oh thanks, Mr. Sun for your warmth and your glow
    For when you appear, you make everything grow.
    The birds sing their songs to begin the new day;
    Enjoying the freshness morning dew brings our way;
    How truly wonderful life is on the plains.

3.   At the end of the day, as the evening begins,
    The sun's lovely rays fill the skies as it dims.
    So goodbye to the day, all its splendor and life;
    As the moon and the stars begin lighting the night;
    How truly wonderful life is on the plains.

4.   How peaceful the stars all twinkle so bright;
    Then quietly at dawn, they start fading from sight.
    When the sun takes the place of the moon once again;
    With a new day we'll start it all over again;
    How truly wonderful life is on the plains.

Chapter 3

Fall

Speedy Jo and her friends were playing when Speedy's mom called for her to come home. Home being your own corner of the vast, endless plains.

"Hi Mom! What's up?"

"Well hon, it's fall and we will be heading into winter. We are going to start to move toward the basin where we will spend the best part of the winter."

Everything was changing on the plains. The drying grass smelled like ripening grain fields, turning the plains a brown-gray and golden color. The yucca along hillsides and the pines were the only color of green. The big sage still held on to its summer color with yellow flowers at its top. Prickly pear cactus patches added a shade of blue-green into the gray and yellow of the drying grasses.

Speedy had all kinds of questions of what winter was. All Mom said was, "I just hope it is a mild one."

Fall was a windy time. Wind, wind, and more wind, with small rain storms and sleet. Down by the creek the cottonwoods, elms, willows and wild plums were putting on their fall colors of gold, red, brown and rust. The leaves rustled in the wind. Many floating gently to the ground, covering the bank and landing in the water. They were quickly carried away. Water snakes and a few garter snakes were lying in the sun along the banks of the creek. They were taking advantage of the last of the warm days left before denning time. Here and there along the creek, several muskrats were busy harvesting their winter store. Raccoon tracks were imprinted in the mud along the creek banks. Fish were starting to gather in the deeper pools. A weasel poked its head out of a hole in a fallen tree, took a quick look around and then darted for a brush pile nearby. A doe mule deer and her fawn hastily drank from the creek, then took flight up a draw. A bear had crossed the creek earlier; his tracks led straight to the wild plum trees. Fall was here to stay, and winter hid right around the corner.

Speedy and her pals were playing and having such fun. The cool days and nights gave them added energy to play tag up and down the bluffs and hills. Running through the beautiful Indian paint-brush with its fiery color; swinging under the chokecherry trees in orange dress; and around a lonesome cottonwood in gold; added beauty and color to the brown and yellow earth of the gullies and bluffs.

Speedy's mom always watched them playing so no one got hurt. Old Aunt Myrt came up to Speedy's mom for a visit.

"Hi Myrt!" said Speedy's mom. "How are you?

"Oh, you know how it is when you get to be my age."

"Well, I really don't," said Speedy's mom. They both laughed.

Aunt Myrt said, "I hope it is going to be a nice, open winter. My old bones can't take a bad cold one."

"Oh Myrt, you old toughie. You can handle anything."

"Well, I hope you're right, dear niece. The march to the basin can be a long one."

"Oh Myrt, you'll be waiting for us when we get there."

"That's a nice thought, niece. Well, I better run along. Tell Speedy I said hi!"

"I will," said Speedy's mom. Off went Aunt Myrt. Speedy's mom thought her aunt seemed to be worried.

Fall brought the rut. Male pronghorn, mule deer, buffalo and elk were putting on their show, battling for dominance, nature's way of securing each kind its future generations. Mother earth and some of her creatures were getting ready for winter's sleep. The fall moon rose in the east, a huge almost perfect round mass of orange. Speedy was so taken by this sight; she found beauty in almost everything.

Early one morning, Ming, the leader of the band, gathered everyone together and said, "It is time to head for the basin. No questions asked!"

Away they went. Off to the left of the column was a huge prairie dog town. As far as the eye could see, the dogs were chirping and barking warnings to the passing column. A burrowing owl poked its head out of his hole to take a look. Then quickly ducked back down into the safety of its burrow. Later that day, other bands joined up. Speedy couldn't believe there were so many of her own kind. Each day the herd grew bigger. Topping a rise, Speedy couldn't believe how far they were strung out—almost out of sight each way she looked.

Thousands of buffalo were everywhere. The march was on. What an unbelievable site this was for Speedy. Countless numbers of elk and mule deer joined in the great migration to the winter range. There was the rumbling of hooves; snorting and bellowing of the buffalo; calls of the elk; bleats of the deer; and snorts of the antelope as though all were talking to one another, making sure all was well. It sounded like a great storm moving across the plains—nature untouched and unspoiled in its natural grand state.

On marched Speedy's column day after day. Late one afternoon, the column came to a sudden stop. Two older antelope almost got into an argument because the one following wasn't watching and butted into the one in front!

In the rear, Speedy Jo and Judy went to see what was stopping their march to the basin. It was a traffic jam all right! I guess you could call it a procession of sorts. It was an endless line of rattlesnakes crossing the trail. The antelope column split and stopped to let them through.

The rattlesnakes were heading for their den. With a rattling-buzzing noise, which seemed to be

endless, they kept coming. They did not want to stop and argue over who could go first, they were in a hurry, and so the antelope herd just waited it out. Finally the last rattler crawled through and didn't even give a thank you!

Oh well. The column started up again. On they marched. Tumble weeds coming out of no where, and being driven by the wind, rolled across the plains as though they were running from something and looking for a place to hide. The temperature dropped in the evenings. They would bed down on the south side of hills or buttes. There was no time for play now. Tension was in the air. Wolves and coyotes were always trailing along beside the big herd.

Speedy asked Mom, "What are they looking for?"

"Oh, they are just doing what nature intended them to do."

"What is nature?" asked Speedy.

"We are nature, hon. You, me, all that you see, smell, eat, all the other animals, the wind, rain, fire, water, grass, brush, trees, just everything around you. We are all a part of nature."

"But Mom, you haven't really explained to me what they are looking for."

"Go to bed. We will talk tomorrow."

"Oh Mom!"

"Go to bed! Tomorrow is going to be another long day."

The next morning they were on the move at sunrise. Not long after they were on the go, Jasper, Speedy's friend, came up and walked with her.

"Boy, Jo, this has sure been a long walk."

"Oh I know. I guess another day or two and we'll be in the basin."

"I sure hope so. I need a good rest."

"Jasper, you're so lazy."

On the outskirts, the coyotes and wolves were still keeping pace with the herd. Speedy could not help wondering what they were doing. Jo spotted Aunt Myrt in a column behind her, and dropped back to her.

"Hi Aunt Myrt."

"Hi Speedy, how are you handling the march?"

"Fine," said Jo. "And you, Aunt Myrt?"

"Well, it is quite trying."

Jo asked, "Why are the coyotes and wolves following us?"

Aunt Myrt said, "They are waiting for me."

"For you, Aunt?" Jo said, shocked. "What are you saying, Aunt?"

"Well young lady, that is just what I am saying. I am saying that they are waiting for me."

"Aunt, you are scaring me."

"Don't be scared, Speedy. That is just the way it is."

"It can't be," said Speedy. "It just can't. Why do they want you, Aunt? Why? Tell me why?"

"Well honey, we spend our days grazing and browsing. They spend their days waiting."

"Waiting for what?" Jo asked.

"Waiting for us. They have to eat too, you know."

"What?" Speedy was in total shock. "You mean, eat us?" she asked.

"Yes dear girl," said Aunt Myrt. "Did you forget the buffalo already?

"No," Speedy said. "I will never forget that as long as I live! Well, they are never going to eat me. Never! And I'm making sure they won't eat you, Aunt Myrt."

"Well, that's a good thought, Speedy. Now you run along."

Speedy caught up with Jasper and told him what Aunt Myrt said. Jasper looked a little sick. Speedy said, "We will have to just be faster than fast and smarter than smart."

Jasper just looked up at the followers with a sick and worried look. It started to snow the following evening. Speedy was in awe. She touched her nose to the snow on the ground and giggled.

Mom said to Jo, "Why are you so silly?"

"It tickles my nose, Mom, and it is cold."

"It will get colder. Now come here and go to bed."

The next day the herd entered the basin. It lay like a giant bowl. It was dotted with trees and willows, and a river ran through it. Other animals were there – buffalo, elk, mule deer, waterfowl bobbed on the river, and birds of all kinds flew over head. It was like a great meeting of all the creatures of creation. Speedy was just in total awe of it all.

Ming came along and took his band out of the main herd and said, "We'll winter over there by that mesa." They all followed. Ming sprang up the mesa and stood guard over his band.

Speedy settled down and rested awhile. Then it hit her. Where was Aunt Myrt? Speedy went to Mom and asked, "Where's Myrt?"

"Aunt Myrt fell behind and didn't come in yet."

"Is she all right, Mom?"

"I'm sure she is, hon."

"Are you sure, Mom?"

"Well, we will see tomorrow."

Chapter 4

Fall and Winter

Jo went and lay down, but could not sleep. She was so worried about Aunt Myrt.

The next morning, long before sunrise, Speedy Jo was up and over getting Jasper to wake up. "Wake up, Jasper. Get up you lazy thing."

"Speedy, what are you doing?"

"Get up and let's go."

"It's still dark."

"I know," said Jo. "We have to go and look for my Aunt Myrt."

"You are crazy, Speedy. We can't go out there by ourselves."

"Yes we can. Let's go."

"No," said Jasper.

"Oh, you chicken. I'll go by myself then."

"Oh, all right Speedy. I'll go too."

On the way out of the basin, they were confronted with Big Mike, a bull bison. "Where are you two young ones going?"

"Out to look for my Aunt Myrt," said Speedy.

"You can't go out there by yourselves. I can't let you. I'm like a guard to the gate you might say," said Big Mike.

"Well, we're going anyway," said Speedy. Jasper said nothing. "No one is going to stop us."

Big Mike said, "I'm coming with you."

"If you want," said Speedy.

Off they went. What a sight! Speedy and Jasper were dwarfed beside Big Mike. Mike said, "What's the rush?"

"I'm Speedy Jo, and I have to find my aunt. She was always there for me, and I'll never let her down, ever. My aunt saved Jasper and me from an old bobcat that was laying in ambush for us. She came charging down this hill and slammed right into Mr. Bobcat and rolled him clear across this small meadow we were playing in. He got up, shocked but bitter, hissed and told Aunt Myrt, 'Come on, try that again, I'm ready for you.' The speed and quickness of my old Aunt was shocking. Mr. Bobcat got rolled again and again. Aunt Myrt was out of control, hacking with her front hooves and screaming, 'That is my niece and her friend, Jasper, you're trying to get. Well buddy, it's not going to happen. Not now or later!' About that time, Annabelle joined in to help Aunt Myrt. They rolled him this way and that, and he finally had enough and took off. Poor old Aunt had to take five after that one."

"Sometimes that can be hard to do," said Big Mike. "You'll have to let the thought be the deed."

Speedy did not answer.

Then Big Mike asked, "Who is Ann-a-belle?"

"Oh, that's one of Aunt Myrt's friends."

"I see," said Mike.

Mike was impressed with Jo. What a caring heart this young lope has!

The sun was coming up when they rounded a butte and there below was Aunt Myrt, lying by a sagebrush, surrounded by wolves, with coyotes waiting in the rear.

Back in the basin, the sun had just risen, and Speedy's mom was in a nervous tremor looking for Jo. "Where's my Jo? Jo, Jo, where are you Jo?"

Jasper's mom came running saying, "I can't find Jasper."

The two mothers were in a complete panic. Then they realized Aunt Myrt had not come in yet. About that time, Ming came down from the mesa. "Not to worry ladies. I saw them head out of the basin with Big Mike. I will go after them."

"We will come too," said the two shaken mothers.

"Come then," said Ming. Off they went.

Speedy, Jasper and Big Mike approached the scene. Speedy started for Aunt Myrt saying, "You get away from my aunt!" The wolves just sneered and the coyotes laughed. "Get away from my aunt."

Aunt Myrt looked up at Speedy with such grateful eyes and worry, and a touch of relief.

"Speedy," Aunt Myrt said. "You crazy little lope, what are you doing here?"

"I came to get you, Aunt Myrt."

About that time, Jasper and Big Mike came on the scene. The sight of Mike changed the expressions on the faces of the wolves and coyotes.

"You heard her," Mike said. "Get, and I mean NOW!"

The wolves and coyotes slowly started to make a retreat, grumbling and complaining as they moved off. One young coyote came up to Speedy. Of all the nerve, thought Speedy.

The young coyote smiled and said, "Hi Speedy, remember me?"

"Eddy?" said Speedy.

"Yes, it is me." The leader of the coyote pack just snarled and gave Eddy a snarling scolding for not leaving with the rest. Eddy ran off to join the pack, almost embarrassed. Head down, he didn't even say good-bye.

This was confusing in a way, as Speedy thought Eddy was her friend last summer. How things change from childhood into adulthood.

About that time, Ming and the two worried mothers showed up. Speedy's mom was in such a frenzy. Jasper just said, "Hi Mom. I'm sorry."

"Oh Jasper," said his mother, "Come here."

"Darn you, Speedy, you scared me to death. What are you doing out here?" said Speedy's Mom.

"I came for my aunt."

"You're going against nature, Speedy."

"I don't care about nature. I only care about my dear aunt. She counts more to me than nature."

"Oh Speedy, what are we going to do with you?"

"Come on Aunt Myrt, let's go home."

"Oh Speedy, you sweet little Lope. I'm very tired, Speedy."

"That's okay Aunt Myrt. We all are. We'll take our time."

Big Mike just smiled. "That Speedy," he said, "she is precious."

Ming walked beside Speedy with such pride. Mom was just full of love for that brave little girl of hers. Even Jasper was showing some pride and his mom was glad just to be with Jasper. Off they headed back to the basin, Speedy walking shoulder to shoulder with Aunt Myrt. Myrt's gratefulness and love for her ever-caring niece just shone all over her for her little Speedy Jo.

Chapter 5

Christmas

The basin was a very homey place to spend the winter. Everyone was keeping busy with their daily needs. Mom was worried about little Speedy Jo because she was all over the place tending to the needy, helping the old and lame. What a strange fawn I have, thought Mom.

One night Mom said, "Why don't you go play with Jasper and the rest of your friends?"

"Oh, I will, but first," Speedy said, "if I can help it, there will never be another buffalo or any creature bad, good, savage or gentle that will be left alone with sickness or lameness or left to die by themselves."

"That's a tall order, Speedy," said Mom.

"I don't care, I'm going to comfort and care for all those in need and that is that!"

It was the first time Speedy stood up to her mom in defense of her own beliefs and ideas. Speedy was growing up.

"Oh Mom, I'm just so happy to help those who are in need. It feels good."

Mom did not and could not come up with anything to answer her.

"Oh Mom, there is old Elmo the buffalo. He is so happy when I show up and giggle and laugh with him. Esther, the lame elk, and I walk together and that makes her so pleased to have someone with her. Jack, the mule deer, has very poor eyesight so I help him go down to the river to drink. He is so grateful. Then there is a mallard duck. His name is George. He has a broken wing, and I am there to help mend it and then . . ."

"Okay, okay," said Mom. "I understand. Now go to bed."

"Oh Mom."

"Go to bed."

"Yes Mom."

This went on day after day. Little Speedy Jo coming in at night very tired and worn out. Mom was beginning to worry about Speedy.

"Speedy," said Mom, "you're just a young lope. You can't keep this up."

"I have to Mom, I just have to. I must help." Sunrise again, and Jo was up and out helping those in need.

Late December, and all fell quiet on the basin. The night was calm and the gentle wind was warm. Everyone was at peace. A bright star shown in the sky. All creatures looked up to witness it. A great calm fell over them all. Over in another land, far away from the basin, a great miracle had taken place a long time before, and all of nature knew of it. Little Jo was taken more than any other, for she had the caring heart. A feeling came over her that she was such a very, very special little lope. As a matter of fact, later that night a little angel said to Speedy, "You are a wonder and you are blessed. For what you do best is to care, little Speedy Jo."

"Me?" asked Speedy. "But I'm just a mere little lope."

"Ah yes, but you have not been missed for we see all," said the little angel. "You are in nature's grace, little Speedy Jo. So take care, and do what you do best and that is to care, little Speedy Jo."

The little angel was just so happy and pleased with herself, that she was the one appointed to tell Speedy that she was so noticed from above; the special little lope with the caring heart. The little angel was so tickled and happy, she just glowed and started to giggle, for she was so happy for Speedy. Her blue eyes sparkled, her auburn hair shown like a bright light, she had a smile from ear to ear. So happy was the little angel. She bent over and gave Speedy a kiss on her head and said, "I must go now, I'm just so happy for you Speedy. I am called Amalia," said the little angel. "Good-bye and take care. I'll be watching over you . . .bye, Speedy."

Poor little Speedy Jo was so taken she could not say a word. Oh, she felt so humble.

Christmas time was so peaceful; all the creatures seemed to take pleasure in the peace it brought.

Chapter 6

Little Speedy Jo's Winter

The winter dragged on, the snows came, and the river froze over. Speedy and her friends would run toward the river, then jump out on the ice and try to slide across to see who could get all the way to the other side. They would laugh and giggle and have such a good time.

Well, one day to their surprise, they slid all the way to the other side of the river and raced up the bank. Then they ran up the slope of a butte, zigzagging around brush and trees, making figure eights, running at each other, then dodging away in the nick of time so as not to run into one another, giggling and laughing all the time. A pair of elk calves asked to join in the fun. Spike and Millie were their names. Three mule deer fawns, by the names of Suzie and Kay, and Kay's brother Elbert, also joined in on the action. What fun they had.

Taking a break, and getting better acquainted, they heard a small grunting sound coming from behind a willow patch. They all wondered what could be making such a sound. Out behind the willows hopped a very small buffalo calf.

"Hi," said the buffalo calf, "my name is Harvey."

Poor Harvey had to be the runt of runts. He also had a bad front leg. He limped when he walked.

Oh my, thought Speedy. The poor little fellow. Speedy introduced everyone. "You are welcome to play with us," said Speedy.

Jasper asked, "What happened to your leg?"

Judy reacted to Jasper's question with embarrassment. "Jasper, you shouldn't ask."

"Oh, that's okay. I was born this way. It is hard for me to keep up with the herd." Harvey became quiet and very sad. Then he said, "My mom left me when I was very young. I guess I was too much of a bother for her. I have been on my own for a long time. I do have a grandmother who kinda watches over me, but she is getting pretty old herself."

"Oh Harvey, you poor fellow," said Speedy.

The rest of the gang became saddened at Harvey's troubled life.

"Come play with us," Judy said.

"Oh, that would be great," said Harvey.

Off they went, with Harvey bobbing and hopping along the best he could. Speedy watched Harvey out of the corner of her eye. Harvey was having fun and felt like he belonged, and according to Speedy, he did.

As hard as the new friends tried, they could not match the speed and quickness of the young lopes, but everyone had a ball. They came charging down the slope, hitting the bank of the river, jumping out as far as they could go, and sliding back across the ice to the other side. Up the bank they flew, crashing in and through the willows to the open prairie, startling several of their neighbors living in the willows. An old jackrabbit by the name of Herman; and his pal Leroy, an elderly cottontail; a pair of meadow larks; two pair of lark buntings; several angry pairs of horned larks; as well as many species of sparrows all evacuated the willow patch when Speedy's gang came crashing through.

The feathered flock just scolded the young lopes and their new pals. Old Herman, who was settling down after his rude interruption, along with his nervous pal Leroy, was about to say something when Speedy, who was so embarrassed, made a very heartfelt apology. "We are so sorry we startled everyone. What can we do to make it right?"

"Oh nothing," said Leroy, which surprised everyone. "I was young once a long time ago. Just run along and we'll get back in order here. You have your fun. It is nice to be young, and you make the most of it."

"Oh thank you," Speedy said. "If you ever need anything, you call for Speedy Jo, okay?"

"That will be fine," Leroy said.

After the neighbors in the willows were settled down and everyone was about to go home, they had forgotten Harvey, who was still on the other side of the river.

Jasper, bless his heart, said, "I'll go get Harvey."

Spike said, "I'll go with you," and off they went.

They all watched as Jasper and Spike helped Harvey back across the ice pack of the river. Harvey bobbing and bouncing along beside Jasper and Spike. All watched with sadness.

Herman the jackrabbit said, "I've seen it all before. The little fellow has heart, they always do. We could learn from them."

When Harvey, Jasper, and Spike reached the bank where the rest of the gang waited, Harvey was all smiles. He was so pleased that they let him play with them.

"We are your friends," said Speedy, "and don't you ever forget that, okay Harvey?"

Harvey said, "I never had any friends before. The other young buffalo snub me, and won't let me play with them because I am different."

Elbert the mule deer fawn said, "You can play with us anytime, Harvey."

They all agreed.

"Oh, that's great," Harvey said. "Well, I guess I better head back to my herd."

So off hopped little Harvey. They all watched him slowly disappear out onto the plains.

Suzie and Kay, the mule deer fawns, said, "I wonder how long Harvey was on the other side of the river?"

"...and all alone," added Millie, the elk calf.

"Poor little fellow," said Judy.

It's so sad, they all agreed. They never saw Harvey again that winter. Not a trace of him.

So, off went Speedy and her pals. All in all, things went well. Spike skinned a knee on a rock by the riverbank, Jasper came up with a sore ankle, and Kay poked an eye on a willow twig. Judy had a small limp but was all smiles. Other than that, everyone came out in good shape. The gang broke up and headed back home. The young elk and mule deer thanked Speedy and her pals for letting them join in on the fun.

Back home that evening, Speedy was so sad and worried about Harvey. Speedy was angry with herself for not bringing Harvey home with her.

"I do hope Harvey will be all right. That poor lonesome little fellow, no one cares about him, and no one wants him." A tear came to Speedy's eyes. How cruel things can be at times. I have so much to learn, thought Speedy.

Speedy's thoughts were of her needy friends; the sick, lame and old. Speedy knew then and for certain what she was to do and be. The cold and snow were hard on the old, and Speedy was always so concerned and worried for them. She made her rounds like clockwork to tend to them.

One day she came across a large herd of buffalo that had moved into the area the day before. Speedy asked a young buffalo named Lou, if she knew of a small crippled calf by the name of Harvey.

"There is no one like that in this herd," said Lou, "Why do you ask?"

"He's a friend of mine," said Speedy, "and I'm so worried about him."

"Well, I can watch for him," Lou said.

"That would be great," said Speedy. "I'll check back later." Speedy felt as though she had totally failed Harvey.

One morning old Elmo didn't want to get up. "It's cold," he said, "and I'm too tired. I'm warm here where I am."

"Are you sure, Elmo?" asked Speedy.

"Yes, Speedy."

Speedy had the feeling she was becoming a pest.

One night the wind picked up and really blew. A blizzard soon followed. The herds and bands grouped together behind bluffs and buttes to get out of harm's way. The storm raged on. No one moved. The snow piled up where it could not blow through. Even the level ground was beginning to become covered now. It never let up.

Animals bedded down with one another, being covered with snow. The wind howled, and the temperature dropped. The snow covered animals looked like humps of anthills in white. Speedy was beside her mom under the blanket of snow.

"Mom, I'm getting hungry and worried about my friends."

"It will let up soon, hon." Soon was a big word on the plains. "In winter we have to stay put

and ride it out, Jo. Don't move so you don't lose your heat under the snow."

Speedy could not get the old and the lame out of her mind. She wondered why we have to get old? Poor Speedy, her patience was about shot. She did not know how much more she could take. The storm raged on. One could go crazy if it didn't let up soon.

Finally, one morning the wind died down and the sun broke through. It was oh so cold! Animals started to stir. The mounds of snow began to move. The buffalo were the first to get going, shaking the snow from them and pawing at the snow, opening up the basin. All others followed. Satisfying hunger was the main event.

Speedy and Mom rose and shook the snow from their coats. Speedy just looked at her white surroundings.

"Let's go over to the rabbit brush and grab a bite. There will be tender grass under the brush," Mom said.

"My nose is cold, Mom."

"I know, hon."

"Mom, I have to check on my friends."

"I think you better wait a bit."

"Oh Mom, look! Here comes Aunt Myrt. Hi Aunt!"

"Oh, hi everyone! Boy, that was a rough one. These old bones could not have taken another day of that torture. A small snack would surely help."

Speedy said, "Here, Aunt Myrt, Mom just cleaned the snow off."

"Oh thank you, Speedy."

Aunt Myrt dove right in. It was a good feeling to have a full stomach again. It warmed one up right quick!

"Mom! Mom!"

"Oh go ahead, check on your friends."

Off went Speedy. Gosh, the snow was deep in spots! Speedy had to find avenues around it all. Jasper was the first.

"Do you want to come with me, Jasper?"

"Oh, I can't. Mom wants me to stay close for a day or so."

"Ok. How's Judy?"

"I don't know. I haven't seen her."

Speedy went on. Elmo the old buffalo was covered with snow but smiling. "Oh Elmo, are you okay!"

"Yes, little Speedy, I'm fine."

"Oh, great!" said Jo. Off she went to Esther the elk. "Hi Esther, how are you?"

"Well believe it or not the leg is better."

"Oh great!" said Speedy.

"Shouldn't you be with your mom Speedy?"

"Well, I had to check on my friends.

The old mule deer, Jack, was standing and just staring. "Jack, are you okay?"

"The snow hurts my old eyes."

"Come with me, Jack. There's some browsing over here for you."

"Well good. I could use a bite," Jack said.

Speedy led Jack to his meal. "Are you going to be okay Jack?"

"I'll be okay, Speedy. You better get back to your mom just in case the wind starts up again." Off went Speedy.

Oh yes, George, my feathered friend, thought Speedy. Down to the river went Speedy.

"George! George!" Up popped George from cattails growing along a seep by the river. "You made it, I see!"

"Oh yes," said George. "The wing is a bit stiff, but better."

"Oh great!" said Speedy. Off pranced Speedy as she headed back home. When she passed Jasper's place, he said, "Still no sign of Judy."

"Let's go look!"

Jasper's mom said, "Oh, okay, but don't be long."

Off they went. They looked, but to no avail. They could not find Judy or Judy's mom or band.

"Gee, I wonder where they went?" asked Jasper.

"I wish I knew," said Speedy.

Night fell quickly and the wind picked up. Speedy and Mom bedded down early. The wind screamed across the basin. A ground blizzard was at its full-blown might. The only way Speedy knew where Mom was laying was by an occasional nuzzle. You could not see the end of your nose, and the temperature dropped fast. This blizzard raged on for two days. The plains in winter can be one of the most dangerous places on earth. But finally it ended and the sun made its appearance once again. The temperature rose slowly and the basin became alive. All creatures were up and about.

Speedy, of course, made her rounds. All was well. This went on and on and Speedy wondered if spring would ever come.

Chapter 7

Spring

Like all things, spring finally made its appearance. Green shoots made a slow but steady show, the air became warmer, the sun shone longer through the day, and the nights became calmer and also warmer. All creatures seemed to become happier and more relaxed. The whole basin became anxious and happy at the same time. Ming came and gathered his band together. "Soon we will head back to our grazing grounds," he said.

As spring moved on, the grass became greener and more lush, and the plains exploded with flowers of every color and kind. Everything was so new and fresh, like the world was being born all over again. Speedy was now a yearling and to her surprise she had a new baby sister by the name of Gin.

"Oh Mom, she is so beautiful!"

Like Speedy at that age, she was all legs, wet, and unsteady. Soon she had her legs under her and away she went with Speedy's careful eye on her. Speedy so loved her little sister that Mom was becoming concerned with Speedy's own welfare. If Speedy wasn't out tending to her needy friends, she was looking after Gin.

One day Mom said, "Speedy, don't worry about Gin. She is in my care as you were at that age."

"But Mom, she is my sister."

"Oh, I know Speedy." Mom paused and sighed, then said, "Speedy, you're going to have to look out for yourself soon, my dear. It's nature's way."

Speedy's thoughts were: Here's the nature thing again.

Finally, one day Ming came and gathered them all together and they started to head out of the basin. Old Aunt Myrt and a lot of other older animals stayed in the basin. For some there was no reason to leave, and some just couldn't. Speedy was just beside herself and so disillusioned.

Aunt Myrt said, "You must go, Jo. I cannot."

"But Aunt Myrt, you have to come with us. You just have to!"

"No," said Aunt Myrt. "I can't, and now you must listen to me, Jo. I've done my share. I've done what nature called on me to do and to be, and now it's time for me to move on."

"On where?" asked Jo.

"On to the next stage."

"Aunt Myrt, you don't make any sense."

"Oh yes," said Aunt Myrt, "I'm going back to nature. Someday you may join me and we'll race the skies together. Take care of the sick and lame, and watch over the needy, for that was what you were born to do."

Old Annabelle showed up. "I'll stay with your Aunt Myrt. We have been friends forever and

there is nothing out there for me anymore either. The basin here is quite nice for us oldies."

Myrt had to laugh. "Us what?" They all had a good laugh.

"Go, Speedy, so you don't get left too far behind." Aunt Myrt gave Speedy a final look. You could see such pride and love in Myrt's old eyes as tears started to show in those big brown eyes. "Now go, remember me if you will, and take care. Now get and leave me alone!" With that, Aunt Myrt slowly turned away.

Speedy slowly left the basin with a tear in her eye and a sad but hopeful heart.

What a surprise! Judy's band showed up and joined them.

"Judy, where were you?"

"Oh, you know. When the blizzard hit, our band moved on south of the basin and that's where we stayed until now."

"Oh Judy. We were so worried about you." Speedy was happy that her friend Judy was safe.

Standing at the entrance of the basin watching the great herds slowly leaving, Speedy caught a glimpse of a bobbing, hopping buffalo calf. She knew right away that it was Harvey. Oh how wonderful! He made it! The sun's rays shown down on the herds as though nature was being blessed from above.

Mom was right, thought Speedy. There is hope. Maybe a little at a time, but it is there. It is all around you. Hope and caring, the two go

together forever and ever. As long as I can, I'll never give up on anyone, Speedy vowed.

So they all left the basin heading their way back to their home range. But Speedy could not get Aunt Myrt and those that were left out of her mind.

Time moved on, but the story of a young antelope's caring heart spread across the plains. She became known as the Princess of the Plains. Lone Eagle chanted and danced and held Speedy in high honor among his people. All creatures, bad and good, savage and gentle, gave way to Speedy when she passed by, for she was the princess of all, the matriarch for those in need.

So run Speedy, run, run, run, for you are so wonderful.

Epilogue

When the old man had finished the story, the owner of the mercantile and his daughters had come to listen. The man and woman by the buggy and Model-T also were there along with a cowboy and a train crew that had dropped off cattle cars by the stockyards. All had been listening to the story of Little Speedy Jo. They were all pleased and quite taken with the story.

The old man stood up and said, "It is getting late. Thank you for listening. It is time for me to head home."

The group broke up and headed in their own directions, back from where they came. All were happy and quiet, thinking about Speedy Jo and her life on the plains. The little girl came up to the old man and thanked him for taking time to tell such a wonderful story. She was so happy, and wanted to know if she could walk the old man home.

"No." He said he would be fine, and that she had better run along home herself.

She said, "Thank you, Mr. Eagle," and off she ran.

So the old man, John Eagle, was his name, great grandson of Lone Eagle, started for his one room abode at the edge of this town that really had no name. He stopped to look at the statue and smiled. He had another story to tell, about how the statue of the antelope came to rest here in this tiny park. That would come later.

Speedy Jo Order Form

Qty	Product Item	Unit Price	Total Price

___ **Speedy Jo, The Antelope Fawn** (Book) $8.95 $ _____
1st in the 3-book series. Speedy Jo learns the
lessons of survival and caring for others in the
prairie's beautiful but harsh environment and
grows to be known as "Princess of the Plains".

___ **Speedy Jo and The Dog Tee** (Book)   8.95 $ _____
2nd in the 3-book series. Travel with Speedy Jo
and Tee through the drought to the Canyon of Hope
as they help other animals through the hard times.

___ **Speedy Jo and the Statue** (Book)   8.95 $ _____
3rd book in the 3-book series. The Warrior of
Truth appears to the prairie inhabitants to prepare
them for the coming of the white settlers.

> *Teacher's Guides available for all Speedy Jo books –*
> *Contact us as shown on the back of this sheet.*

T-Shirts
___ Speedy Jo T-Shirt, Natural Color $12.00 $ _____
     Specify S, M, L, XL _____
___ Blue Heeler T-Shirt, Light Ash Color   12.00 $ _____
     Specify S, M, L, XL _____

Baseball Caps   (One size fits all)
___ Speedy Jo Cap, Black $8.50 $ _____
___ Blue Heeler Cap, Blue   8.50 $ _____

Screensaver
___ Speedy Jo Screensaver $4.95 $ _____
     8 scenes from all three Speedy Jo books
     on 3 ½" floppy disk. PC only.

Stuffed Animals
___ Speedy Jo, The Antelope Fawn. 9" tall $10.00 $ _____
___ Eddy, The Howling Coyote. 12" tall   10.00   _____
___ Harvey, The Buffalo. 10" long   10.00   _____
___ T. J., The Cougar. 9" long   10.00   _____
___ Pete, The Skunk. 10" tall   10.00   _____
___ Ling, the Wolf. 10" long   10.00   _____
___ Boo-Jang, the Bear. 12" tall   14.00   _____
___ Mini Boo-Jang, the Bear. 6" tall   6.00   _____
___ Butch, the Raccoon. 7" tall   6.00   _____

Call for prices on institutional or bulk orders.

Subtotal: $ _____

---

* Shipping & Handling

$2.00 for the first item ordered

$1.25 for each additional item

---

3 % Sales Tax (CO only) $ _____

*Shipping and Handling $ _____

Total Order: $ _____

Payment should be made by check or money order
payable to Blue Heeler Publishing.

Mail To: Blue Heeler Publishing
P.O. Box 1, Carr, CO 80612

Contact us: Phone: (970) 897-2436, (970) 532-1012
Fax: (970) 532-2938
E-mail: writingrancher@verinet.com

Name _____

Address _____

City/State/Zip _____

Phone _____ Email _____

Upcoming Products – Audiotapes (Available approximately 12/1/00)

☐ Please check here if you would like further information on the
price and release date of these audiotapes.

- Speedy Jo Audiotape ·· 5 songs from Book 1
- Speedy Jo and The Dog Tee Audiotape ·· 5 songs from Book 2
- Speedy Jo and The Statue Audiotape ·· 5 songs from Book 3
- Collected Songs of Speedy Jo – all 15 songs

☐ Please sign me up to receive my free Writing Rancher's
twice-a-month e-newsletter. My e-mail address is shown above.